Embers Of Us

Sanjana Reddy Tummala

BookLeaf Publishing

India | USA | UK

Dedication

This book belongs to every broken soul that is longing for closure. I hope you know that even though you were robbed of your time with your melancholic love; I pray that you read this and console your heart, that everything that had happened was for the best and you had your pace. I hope this book helps you move closer to what your heart yearns for and what it couldn't earn before. I pray that you believe so and thrive for the best.

Preface

Love is the most profound paradox of human existence. It is both our greatest strength and our deepest vulnerability. It gives us wings and teaches us the weight of longing. It builds us up, only to sometimes leave us in ruins -- forcing us to rebuild, to reconsider, to rediscover ourselves. It is about intimacy -- the kind that goes beyond touch and words, the kind that lingers even after someone has left.

This book is not just about love in its euphoric state but also about its quite moments, its uncertainties and its endings which are captured in these verses. These poems are not just about love at its peak, but also about its unravelling. They are about intimacy -- the kind that exists beyond the physical, in shared glances and whispered dreams. These series of verses belong to everyone who have dared to love, who have faced the ache of separation, and who have sought meaning in both.

If you have ever loved deeply, if you have ever lost someone and found yourself in the process, this book is for you. May these pages remind you that love, in all its forms, is unconditional and is never wasted.

Acknowledgements

This book is a tapestry woven from many threads, and I am forever grateful to those who contributed their own strands.

To the quiet voices of my past, whose memories I carry with me, and whose presence continues to shape every word I write.

To the landscape of my life, with its mountains and rivers, whose beauty continues to inform my imagination.

To the silence that allows me to hear my own thoughts, and the chaos that urges me to write them down.

To my family, who have walked this path with me, both in person and in spirit—thank you for the light you've brought into my life.

Mirror! mirror! on the wall, who is the saddest of them all?

Staring through the soft pastels surrounding her castle,
she lives with a **grim past**.

Though she cannot stand a speck of dust around,
she brims with **agony** and restless fragments of **hate**.

There she lies on her porch, gazing at the bright sun and
muddy lilies — all while **leering**, a quiet **Manichean**.

The voices are faint, yet they **antagonize** her fear of
loneliness.

Staring into the mirror, she sees the reflection of her
ashen thoughts
etched deep in her sunken eyes —
even as the silvered frame begs her to embrace a rare
sight:

the velvet gaze of her *toffee eyes,*
her *flustered, flame-kissed cheeks,*
and the *sapphire seam* of lips like dew-drenched petals.

2. The Quiet Resistance

She was grateful for what the crowd chose to see,
for all the pain and jeopardy she hid —
pretension her weapon, pain the poison she endured.

Green pastures stretched for acres and beyond,
but her mind lingered on the parasites beneath.

She never cared for unsolicited thoughts,
yet was grateful for their **transparency** within the
bewilderment.

Walking through the shrubs, she prayed for the flowers
to bloom.
All her hopes turned nigh when the bloom resisted the
night.

She found warmth in the quiet bloom —
a flower unfolding in a gentle tune.

In the petals' hush, the world stood still;

life's presence lingered — *calm and real.*
No rush, no race — just time unfurled,
a fleeting moment, yet whole and full.

3. The Thicket of Temptation

Her calmness was as serene as settled dust before the
storm —
an irksome void she never knew existed.

The moment she dared to wonder,
she was caught in a labyrinth of illusions.

Gazing into her despondent eyes,
they implored the goddesses to take pity
on her spiraled self, as her senses unraveled like never
before.

*"Of all the battle cries I bellowed in silence,
what was it that seized your keenness?"* she pondered.

Glaring at her restless heart, sensing a new bloom,
they laughed at her puerility — *melodiously.*

**"A new storm brews upon your shore —
not of anguish, not of war.**

**No trail of fire, no test of might — but of *Eros*," they
tittered.

"Do you still wonder?
If your thoughts remain nigh,
the **Forest of veil** awaits your presence.

But beware: with each step, the forest will whisper back
—

not in words, but in the actions of your own mind.

So tread lightly.
Desires, once freed, do not return untamed," they
warned.

4. Trance of the Timber

Curious of the secrets the forest keeps,
she stepped within, where *twilight sleeps.*

Though her mind would often stray,
black roses lured her back to stay.

Lifeless branches appeared **sable** and feeble, yet
giants of trees stood in the shadows **bold.**

She wandered deep where *silence weeps,*
their twisted forms, a *frozen scene.*

Souls ensnared beneath the trees,
chains like roots in earth's embrace,
trapping whispers, *time erased.*

Hollow trunks ferry *voiceless cries,*
haunted by their **captive sighs.**

Curious and curiouser, she walked in deep.

5. The Wicked Wisp

Echoes of goddesses' conundrum rang in her mind,
a silent prayer to shun the whirling abyss.

Feigning indifference, yet longing inside,
for fate to turn and worlds to collide.

Through tangled woods, her footsteps strayed,
where secrets in shadows softly swayed.

Then, before her — still and wide,
a lifeless pond, like time denied.

She called into its hollow deep,
no voice to wake, no soul to weep.

She reached to the silent deep,
but the water recoiled, as if in grief.

Like a ghost afraid of mortal skin,
it shrunk away, refusing within.

She was determined, bold, fixated,
yet once more, the waters rolled.

Sinking, shrinking, just out of grasp,
like time itself slipping past.

A force unseen, a secret unfold,
a pond that shunned her touch — ice-cold.

6. Beneath the Veil of Quiet Reverence

Though she wandered the forest alone,
its rejection cut her deeper than stone,
a pain foreseen, rejection earned before,
but an unforeseen touch of **hate**.

Silent echoes filled her space,
yet the forest denied her grace.

For the first time, she had learned of the shivers;
fear took hold of her.

Lost among the withered souls and branches,
trapped in cold.

Alone she stood, yet *safe* somehow.

Stagnant thoughts and sterile mind,
Helpless, she stood, as silence swayed.

Once a nonchalant realm, entranced by the inescapable
femininity and shared reverie,
there lay a **pearl of dread** in darkness as she spilled a tear
in silver streams.

7. A Verdant Soul

The moment her teardrop kissed the earth,
the forest stirred, alive with birth.

Sunken souls whispered through the trees,
as rippling waters rose to her.

The lilies waltzed, their petals wide,
yearning for her, a glowing guide.

The stones below, with whispered grace,
shifted to form a resting place.

The weeping weeds, in waters deep,
stirred awake from ancient sleep.

They danced, transformed in colors bright,
scaled souls born of liquid light.

One arose, so soft, so rare,
a **pearl in fins** — *a gift as a souvenir* for her to bear.

8. The Glee of Gossamer Dreams

She felt **conceited** by the sudden revelations,
yet *elated about the synergy made.*

She wondered,
"Why hide such **ethereal** *facade?*
What made you reckon to persevere with such *silent dread?*

Why did you not reveal the truth you kept so long concealed?"

Casting off their camouflage,
the realm of flora and fauna exhaled the weight of the world,
while **waters shunned.**

"We've seen deceit, we've known disguise,
too many times, with trusting eyes."

"The mortal world has played its part,
with empty oaths and hollow hearts.

So in this realm of doubt and night,
we hid ourselves from tainted light."

9. A Wish Woven in Silence

She took the pearl, both as a blessing and
a gift—
A whispered secret the waters keep.
With quiet breath, she dared to say,
"What does the future weave my way?"

The scaled souls swirled in silver streams,
Their voices soft as drifting dreams:
"The path ahead is yours to mold;
What you desire, the future holds.
Hold the pearl within your hand—
Speak your wish within your heart.
But doubt—beware—for if it sways,
Your darkest fears shall shape the days."

She clutched the pearl with trembling grace;
A shadow flickered on her face.

"I do not wish to leave," she sighed,
"For here, my heart feels safe inside."

The rocks beneath her shuddered low—
A warning hummed in undertow:
"To linger long in comfort's keep
Is but to drift where lost souls weep.

For those who stay and fear the tide
Will never know the dawn's divide.

Purgatory, though soft and bright,
Blurs the line 'tween day and night."

10. In the Shadow of Tomorrow

She stood stoic, like an ancient trunk,
rooted in place, unsure of the undefeated path.

With a borrowed breeze, she gathered her mettle,
prepared to tread the path into the beyond.

Holding the pearl as if it were her breath itself,
she whispered, "I want to walk forward, unburdened and
bold."

The creatures spoke, their voices calm yet firm:
**"Before you move forward, know this—you are not
alone.**
Another soul lingers in this world,
trapped between the echoes of his past and the weight of
his fate,
awaiting release from the madness this realm has carved
into him."

"Him?" she breathed, her eyes alight with a sudden,
fierce hope,
her cheeks blooming like the ripest cherries kissed by
the sun.

A surge of emotions, foreign and wild, swept through
her,
but before she could surrender to the storm within,
reality's sharp edge pulled her back,
leaving her breathless, uncertain, yet awake.

She asked, *"Why can't I stay here, be your neighbor, and*
find peace?"

The beings answered, their voices deep with knowing,
"There is only the present and the future in this
wilderness.
The present is what you run from,
and the future is what you run toward—
a way to escape the weight of the past.
In any circumstance,
you must make a move."

11. Beneath the Waiting Sky

She gripped the relic of her destiny, *quivering with urgency,*
seizing its presence as if it were the key she desperately sought.

A rush surged through her chest—wild, relentless—
a storm of longing, of uncertainty, of something unnamed.

What is this yearning
that tugs at her like the restless tide?

She shut her eyes,
lost in the depths,
seeking an answer in the silence.

There she stood, on barren land within the heart of the forest,
a world draped in monochrome—silent, endless, still.

And yet, for the first time, she felt close to home,
a strange comfort settling in her chest,
as if the emptiness itself had been waiting for her.

The branches hung low, twisted and bare,
*their skeletal fingers stretching in shades of white and
black.*

The wind whispered through the leaves,
a ghostly swoosh, neither warm nor cold,
just a quiet echo of something long forgotten.

With constant rehearsals of endurance,
her mind wandered still,
searching through the quietude
for a presence unseen—
the one the scaled beings had spoken of.

A quiet longing stirred beneath her thoughts,
a summons she could not explain,
as if the very air carried traces of someone
just beyond her reach,
clinging, lost in the same endless hush.

12. Thrum Beneath, Ether Above (Part 1)

Amidst the land so bare and stark,
she found a bloom in endless dark.

A patch of holly, bright yet lone,
bloomed upon a soil of ashen stone.

With wary steps, she knelt to witness
a sight so strange, a mystery.

Her fingers reached—but fate withdrew,
as thundered words the silence slew.

"Touch them not," the warning came,
a voice like echoes wrapped in flame.

Its weight, like waves against the shore.
A breath—a gasp—her world spun tight,
as fear embraced her in her thrum.

The pearl fell loose, her senses sank,
and to the ground she descended.

13. Thrum Beneath, Ether Above (Part 2)

He lifted her with **tender urgency**,
his bare hands cradling her fragile form,
Galloping through the wild breath of the wind,
toward the river's shimmering charm.

The horse's hooves sang a hurried hymn,
the earth blurring beneath their flight.
While she, tethered to the haze of her *fading senses*,
felt the pull of *fading light.*

Confusion swirled, a tempest fierce,
yet something *soft* began to rise—
A warmth that bloomed from deep within,
as his embrace wrapped 'round her ties.

His arms, a **fortress**, strong and sure,
held her close, heart to heart,
Secure against the world's fierce roar,
a tender symphony, a sacred art.

Her heart beat wild, a restless drum,
stirred by the rhythm of his care,
A strange, sweet ache from soul to soul,
woven in the *breath of air.*

In that fleeting, stolen moment,
beneath the sky's vast, endless dome,
She found herself *lost*—and yet—
she knew she'd found her way back **home**.

14. In the Midst of the Haze

Reaching the river's trembling edge,
He laid her down, a fragile pledge,
Sprinkled water, cool and clear,
Hoping—*praying*—for her to hear.

She stirred, as if the world was shy,
Eyes averted, avoiding his sky.
Embarrassment tucked behind her gaze,
A silent story, lost in a haze.

Yet he, with care, sought her eyes,
Measuring if faintness still lies.
His voice, a whisper, soft and true,
Breathed words only meant for you:

"Your eyes—like swan's, serene and deep,
Your skin, as soft as butter's sweep.
Your hair—a honeysuckle's grace,
Nature's art in one sweet face."

Forgive my bluntness, if you please,
I lose my wits when beauty's tease
Is woven in the breath of air,
A fleeting moment, *rare and rare.*

15. Beneath the Guise, a Thread of Truth

Her heart stirred, yet her guard held strong,
Impressed, but wary, she played along.
"How come you're alone, with no soul in sight,
No creature, no shadow, no flicker of light?"

He chuckled, a tease in his voice,
"It's just you and me — *what a choice."*

She met his gaze, sharp and clear,
"I see you waste no time, I fear."

His smirk grew, bold and bright,
"When I find what God has made just right,
Something I alone deserve to keep,
I'll make every effort, my promises deep."

She looked away, her cheeks aglow,
Blushing softly, her heart a quiet flow.

Though gratitude bloomed, soft and bright,
A shadow lingered in her light.

Her heart whispered, a quiet plea,
"Not all is as it seems to be."

A gut instinct, sharp and clear,
Echoed louder than any fear.

She watched his words, each one spun,
A thread of truth, a trace undone.

Her gaze swept wide, the land, the air,
Every rustle, every whispered care.

For in his charm, beneath the guise,
She sensed a puzzle, wrapped in lies.

Yet still, she stayed, heart tightly wound,
A mystery in him yet unbound.

Grateful, yes, but wary too,
For not all paths lead straight and true.

16. Flowers in a Haystack

He led her to a mansion vast,
Its walls like whispers from the past.
No windows pierced its stoic face,
A fortress carved in time and place.
Like motte and bailey, strong and old,
A silent story, bold yet cold.

"Rest," he said, his voice a thread,
"I'll return when supper's spread."

She lowered her gaze, heart light yet taut,
Curiosity stirred her sanctum's thought.

She wandered halls where shadows stayed,
Where echoes of the past were laid.
The air was thick, untouched, unseen,
As if the walls held secrets keen.

He returned, his voice a gentle call,
Echoing softly through the mansion's hall.

She stepped to the porch, heart unaware
Of the surprise woven in evening air.

There he stood, with a garden vast,
Petals blushing, colors cast—
In his arms, a bloom-filled sea,
A portrait painted just for me.

"I've gathered each flower, wild and true,
To mirror the beauty I see in you.
Every hue, every scent, every graceful sway,
Reflects the magic you bring to my day."

Her breath caught, a quiet sigh,
As stars blinked softly in the sky.
For in that moment, pure and bright,
He held her heart within the light.

17. Like a Moth to the Flame

"What do you seek in me?"
She faced him, her heart fluttering with uncertainty.

*"My frays soar high through my skin," she confessed,
"and I dare not place myself beside these fragile lilies,
their grace far beyond my own."*

He met her gaze with quiet intensity, his voice like a
soothing breeze.

"You are crafted, woven with all that I lack," he said,
"vested in the gifts nature has bestowed, for *it makes no
mistakes.*
*These flowers do not yearn to be plucked,
unless they have made peace with the thorns they bear,
with the unseen parasites that cling to their stems.*

*And as they age, their most precious parts fall away—
the petals wither,* but still, they hold their beauty.
For the greatest lesson lies not in what we lose,

but in how we see ourselves."

His gaze softened as he reached out, tenderly brushing
her hand.

"I seek the generosity in you,
as you caress the blooms you hold so gently.
I seek the femininity you wear, graceful and unshaken.
I seek the warmth that my soul craves,
the kind that draws me to you,
like a moth helplessly drawn to the flame—
my love, my heart, my fire."

18. To Surrender, In the Arms of Duality

The sigh she bore was like a curse lifted from her soul,
a weight she never knew she carried until his arms
devoured her entirely.

The echo of his words — **my sweet sweet briar** —
lingered in her mind,
whispering through the day, humming through the
night,
until it became the only rhythm she knew.

In his presence, her **cynicism dissolved,**
and she wrapped herself around him,
as though surrendering to something she'd long denied.

She spoke, her voice a tender confession:
"A feeling I never thought I'd be capable of bearing...
the zeal to live now thrives within me, *stronger than*
ever.
You are the source of my joy and my sorrow,

and I will make peace with this duality,
for I have longed for this embrace,
and now I know I am willing to commit any sin,
if it means making us one forever."

19. My Sweet Briar, My Redemption

What pulls your presence here? What keeps you grounded forever?
A man of your gravitas — a flame where all eyes are drawn, she asked.

**I refused to learn the same lesson too many times.
I craved diamonds but never cherished them enough to keep them shining forever.
I craved gold but never intended to protect it.
I craved all things of value around me,
but never paid the price — and over time,**
my worth grew too poor to carry them still.

I witnessed disdain, loathing, abhorrence, and revulsion
—

the price for my actions.

I prayed, and let out a wound of sound in search of forgiveness.

You, my sweet, sweet briar —
you are the cure for my sacred ache.

I pray you find trust, love, and regard in us.

20. An Empty Vase of Oleanders

My mind craves chaos when I am at peace,
My soul yearns for solitude, though love is bestowed
upon me.

Though my body is sculpted by nature,
I have turned to stone, so as not to witness the scars
engraved.

I am merely a being of the lost cosmos;
the skin I bear would even make a molting serpent
recoil.

My irises mirror brown, muddied waters,
and my constant self-loathe makes my bones fragile,
tumbling into the depths of sorrow's cries.

No creature of grace would dream of my shell,
crevices etched with the ink of self-doubt and
worthlessness.

Even my dear oleander never dares to grow where my
footsteps crawl.

21. To Be Held, To Be Home

Tears roll down his dear cheek,
unaware of the pain she constantly carried.

Your shell is a cloak of stone,
made to hold both the best and worst of you
as you fight your battles.

Your skin is velvet—born of soil and sunlight,
as if spun from the marrow of ripe avocados and golden
rain.

When sunlight showers you,
your eyes resemble the last light of golden hour,
burnt caramel beneath the moonlight.

I shall fill every void you carry,
and pour myself into every crevice you keep.
I crave to be one with you—forever.

It would be cowardly of me not to admit

the fear of staying too long,
but your femininity reminds the man in me
of my forever duties.